P9-CRX-161

CANADIAN HISTORY TIMELINES

The Building of the Canadian Pacific Railroad

Blaine Wiseman

Weigl

Published by Weigl Educational Publishers Limited
6325 – 10 Street SE
Calgary, Alberta, Canada
T2H 2Z9

Website: www.weigl.ca

Library and Archives Canada Cataloguing in Publication data available upon request.

ISBN 978-1-4872-0021-3 (hardcover)
ISBN 978-1-4872-0022-0 (softcover)
ISBN 978-1-4872-0023-7 (multi-user eBook)

Printed in the United States of America in North Mankato, Minnesota
1 2 3 4 5 6 7 8 9 0 18 17 16 15 14

052014
WEP130514

We acknowledge the financial support of the Government of Canada through
the Canada Book Fund for our publishing activities.

Photograph Credits
Library and Archives Canada: 4-5, 7, 13, 15, 20-21, 25, 27, 28-29, 30
Getty Images: 3, 4-5, 7, 8-9, 11, 13, 15, 16-17, 18-19, 22-23, 24-25, 26-27, 30

Project Coordinator
Aaron Carr

Art Director
Terry Paulhus

CONTENTS

The Builders

Canada is the second-largest nation in the world. It covers 9,976,140 square kilometres. This land is so large that it is divided into six **time zones**. More than 35 million people live here. Millions of people settled this vast country because of the railroad. The Canadian Pacific Railway (CPR) united the country from the Atlantic to the Pacific coasts.

JOHN A. MACDONALD

John A. Macdonald was Canada's first prime minister. His primary goal was to unite the country. With so much land, he knew building a railway would bring the country closer together.

DONALD SMITH

Fur trader Donald Smith came to Canada to work for the Hudson's Bay Company (HBC). He quickly rose up the ranks to become principal shareholder. Smith then helped form the Canadian Pacific Railway Company, and later entered politics.

WILLIAM CORNELIUS VAN HORNE

William Cornelius Van Horne was another successful American businessman. He completed the railway and opened the Canadian West to tourism and business.

"The biggest things are always the easiest to do because there is no competition."
William Cornelius Van Horne

British Columbia would only agree to become part of Canada if a railroad were built to link the provinces.

A New Nation

Before becoming a nation, Canada was a French **colony**. France was not the only country to seek control of lands that would later become Canada. Great Britain also wanted access to the many natural resources that this land offered. For this reason Great Britain established the Hudson's Bay Company (HBC) in 1670. This company controlled a huge territory called Rupert's Land. By 1763, Great Britain took control of former French territory in Canada, making it a British dominion. This included large parts of modern-day Quebec, Ontario, Manitoba, Saskatchewan, Alberta, and Nunavut.

Canada became a nation on July 1, 1867. Its official name was the Dominion of Canada. John A. Macdonald became the prime minister. The new country was made up of Ontario, Quebec, New Brunswick, and Nova Scotia. Rupert's Land and British Columbia were still separate territories, along with Newfoundland and Prince Edward Island. Prime Minister Macdonald wanted the nation of Canada to reach from the Atlantic Ocean to the Pacific Ocean. However, there was another country trying to control the land.

In 1867, the Grand Trunk Railway was the world's largest railroad. It crossed Ontario and Quebec, extending into the United States.

Canada's first prime minister was born in Scotland. He came to Canada as a child.

Around the time of **Confederation**, the United States was expanding across North America. Hundreds of thousands of Americans were settling the West, in California and the Oregon Territory. Shortly before Confederation, the United States bought Alaska from Russia. Now, the United States wanted Rupert's Land in order to control the vast **majority** of the continent. The Canadian government did not want that to happen, nor did Great Britain.

Rupert's Land was given to the Hudson's Bay Company (HBC) by Great Britain in 1670. After 200 years, the fur trade was no longer a strong industry. The HBC could not afford to keep the territory. They decided to sell Rupert's Land. The United States paid $7.2 million for Alaska, and the country would pay more for Rupert's Land.

Instead, the British government bought Rupert's Land back from the HBC for $1.5 million. The British gave it to Canada. It was a great bargain for Canada. It owned the land, but it did not control the land just yet.

"I would be quite willing, personally, to leave that whole country a wilderness for the next half-century but I fear if Englishmen do not go there, Yankees will." John A. Macdonald

Rupert's Land changed hands several times in the 17th and 18th centuries. It was eventually given to Canada by Great Britain.

Settle Your Differences

Rupert's Land was mostly populated by Aboriginal peoples. The explorers and fur traders travelled west by foot, canoe, and wagon. They often relied on Aboriginal peoples as guides and built strong relationships with them. Many fur traders started families with the Aboriginal peoples and created the **Métis** nation.

The Métis had lived in Rupert's Land for generations, building the Red River Settlement near Hudson Bay. They believed the land belonged to them. With more and more settlers arriving from Canada, the Métis felt threatened. Led by Louis Riel, they rebelled. They refused to give up their land.

Prime Minister Macdonald sent Donald Smith to **negotiate** with the Riel government. Smith told Riel the Métis could keep their land, language, and culture if they joined Canada. Before they agreed to the treaty, Smith helped them make a list of their rights. On July 15, 1870, the Red River Settlement became Manitoba, the fifth Canadian province. Canada was expanding.

1869

1867   1869   **1870**   1870–1871   1872–1873   1873–1880

When Manitoba became a province, the rest of Rupert's Land became known as the Northwest Territories. This included large parts of modern Manitoba and the Northwest Territories, as well as Saskatchewan, Alberta, Yukon, and Nunavut.

This drawing shows a French Métis from the 19th century. The Métis were a mix of First Nations Aboriginal groups and European settlers.

John A. Macdonald's dream of uniting Canada from the Atlantic coast to the Pacific coast was beginning to come true. With Rupert's Land under Canadian control, the prime minister turned his attention to British Columbia. The people of British Columbia knew Macdonald was eager to have them join Canada. This gave them an advantage in negotiations with the Canadian government.

In June 1870, politicians from British Columbia met with the Canadian government in Ottawa. The Canadians agreed to almost all the demands of the British Columbians. Canada agreed to take over the colony's **debt** and also gave British Columbia strong **representation** in the federal government.

The most important part of the agreement did more to unite Canada than anything else. The Canadian government agreed to build a railway linking the West with the rest of Canada. Macdonald promised to complete the railway within 10 years. Now it was time to get to work.

John A. Macdonald had a long and successful political career. He even overcame being forced to resign as prime minister due to his role in the Pacific Scandal.

A Train Wreck

After British Columbia joined the Confederation, there was an **election** and Macdonald won in a close call. He continued planning the railway and hired Sir Hugh Allan to build it.

The decision to hire Allan hurt Macdonald dearly. Allan had donated more than $350,000 to Macdonald's election **campaign**. Most of this money came from Allan's American business partners. In return for the donations, Macdonald gave Allan the **contract** to build the CPR.

When the **opposition party** and Canadian press found out about the deal, the Pacific Scandal began. Canadians were angry with the prime minister. It was illegal to give Allan the CPR contract in exchange for campaign donations. Citizens were also angry that Macdonald and Allan had taken money from American businessmen.

Macdonald's election win came at a great personal cost. By the end of 1873, John A. Macdonald was in deep trouble. He resigned as prime minister. Hugh Allan's company never started building the Canadian Pacific Railway.

1867   1869   1869–1870   1870–1871   1872
1873   1873–1880

"I trust that it may be said of me in the ultimate issue, 'Much is forgiven because he loved much,' for I have loved my country with a passionate love." John A. Macdonald

Hugh Allan had a successful shipping business. Allan had never built a railroad when he received the CPR contract.

Back on the Rails

The new Canadian government put railway building on hold. Frustrated by broken promises, British Columbia threatened to leave the Confederation and join the United States. The Canadian government wanted British Columbia to remain part of Canada. To do this they began construction of the railroad, but progress was slow.

After five years, Canadians were ready to give Macdonald another chance. He won the 1878 election and returned to power. Once again, as prime minister, Macdonald set his sights on building the railway. Time was running out on his deadline. He wanted to convince the people of British Columbia that he was serious about his promise.

In 1880, construction on the western part of the railway began in Port Moody, British Columbia. It would run from the West Coast, through the mountains, and link to the railway being built from the East. Macdonald's grand project was back on track, but he still needed more money to complete it.

1873

1867   1869   1869–1870   1870–1871   1872–1873   1880

Many men who worked on the western section of the railway were gold miners. They arrived in British Columbia during the Cariboo Gold Rush in the 1860s.

This ship contains the first load of iron that would be used on the Canadian Pacific Railway. Building the railroad was a massive undertaking, but it would eventually unite all of Canada.

Full Steam Ahead

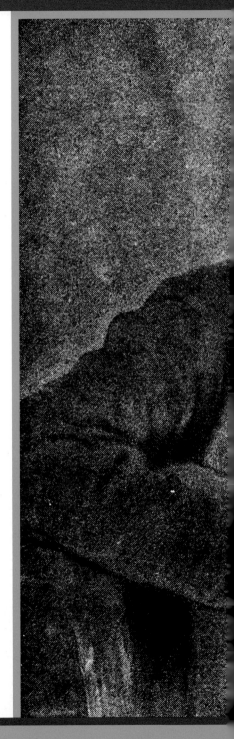

Canada needed business partners. In 1880, some Canadian businessmen contributed money to start a new railway company. The group was led by two cousins, George Stephen and Donald Smith. Stephen was a successful banker and railway president. Smith was well known for the Red River Rebellion where he successfully negotiated for Rupert's Land from Louis Riel. He also helped topple John A. Macdonald by voting to censure government during the Pacific Scandal. Together, Stephen and Smith had saved a failing railway before. The prime minister knew these were the men for the job.

On February 16, 1881, the Canadian Pacific Railway Company was formed. Canada gave the company $25 million. In addition, Canada gave 10 million hectares of land on which to build the railway.

After a slow start, William Cornelius Van Horne was hired to lead construction in the East. Van Horne was very confident, promising to lay more than 800 kilometres of track the first year. Though flooding on the prairies delayed work, crews almost met Van Horne's goal. They laid 673 km of mainline track in the summer of 1882, an incredible accomplishment. The railroad was well on its way.

1867   1869   1869–1870   1870–1871   1872–1873   1873–1880

Sir Sandford Fleming was frustrated that each town along the tracks set its clocks to a different time. He helped develop a system of standardized time that split the world into different time zones.

George Stephen was a business partner and first cousin to Donald Smith. The two worked together to create the Canadian Pacific Railway.

1880

1882

1882–1885

1884–1885

1885

1885–1891

1891–TODAY

19

Meanwhile in British Columbia, construction crews were working east through the Rocky Mountains. Cutting through the mountains was difficult, dangerous work. There were few workers available in British Columbia, so the Canadian Pacific Railway Company had to find them somewhere else.

The man in charge of the railway's western section was Andrew Onderdonk. Wanting to save money, Onderdonk hired the cheapest workers he could find. Thousands of Chinese workers came to Canada to build the railroad. These workers were paid only $1 per day and had to buy their food and camping equipment. Canadian workers made between $1.50 and $2.50 per day, and they did not have to pay for food or lodging.

Chinese workers were given the most difficult, dangerous jobs. They used explosives to blast tunnels through the mountains and built bridges across raging rivers. Landslides, avalanches, and dynamite blasts were constant dangers. Without money to buy fresh fruit and vegetables, many Chinese also died of scurvy. The hard work and sacrifice of these Chinese workers played a major role in uniting Canada.

1867   1869   1869–1870   1870–1871   1872–1873   1873–1880

Nearly 17,000 Chinese men worked on the CPR between 1881 and 1885. At least 600 of them died from the work.

Life on the railway was especially hard for Chinese workers. Many returned to China when the line was completed.

Workers blasted through the Rocky Mountains and laid tracks across the prairies. Smith and others with the Canadian Pacific Railway Company knew people would move west with the railroad, so they began selling land to settlers. The prairie land surrounding the tracks was excellent farmland. The Canadian Pacific Railway Company advertised this land to settlers and immigrants who wanted to start a new life in the West. They recruited people from Eastern Canada and even Europe.

In 1884, the Canadian Pacific Railway Company chose 10 farms to **showcase** prairie farming. Trains loaded with crops from these experimental farms travelled around Ontario and Quebec. The company hoped to attract Eastern Canadians to farm on the prairies. As more people moved west, they built communities near the train tracks. Hundreds of new towns formed close to the CPR route and grew into cities.

Settlement was unwelcome news for the Aboriginal peoples. Once again, they felt their land was being taken away from them. Louis Riel, who had been sent into a five-year **exile** for his role in the Red River Rebellion, returned to lead a second rebellion. The government needed to send the military to the Northwest Territories quickly. Using the railway, thousands of troops, led by the North-West Mounted Police, travelled to crush the North-West Rebellion.

"Late events have shown us that we are made one people by that road, that iron link has bound us together in such a way that we stand superior to most of the shafts of ill-fortune." John A. Macdonald

The Niagara Bridge was built to carry the Grand Trunk Railway between Canada and New York.

1884

1885

1880–1882   1882–1885   1885   1885   1885–1891   1891–TODAY

The North-West Rebellion convinced Canadian politicians how important the railroad was. It could quickly move troops and equipment to keep peace across the vast country. The government decided to provide the money needed to finish building the CPR.

Van Horne and his crews quickly moved across the prairies, while Onderdonk's crews continued work through the mountain passes. On November 7, 1885, the two sections of track finally met at Craigellachie, British Columbia. Workers and leaders gathered at the town in the Eagle Pass. They celebrated completion of the world's longest railway. Donald Smith was given the honour of driving the last **spike** of the Canadian Pacific Railway.

Though Prime Minister Macdonald failed to keep his 10-year promise of 1871, it was still an extraordinary achievement. From the time the CPR became official in 1881, Canada's transcontinental railway was built in less than five years. Macdonald's dream of uniting Canada from coast to coast had finally come true.

1867   1869   1869–1870   1870–1871   1872–1873   1873–1880

"All I can say is that the work has been well done in every way." William Cornelius Van Horne

Donald Smith drives the last spike into the Canadian Pacific Railway in Craigellachie, British Columbia. The railway was finished.

1880–1882

1882–1885

1884–1885

1885

1885–1891

1891–TODAY

25

Stops along the Way

The first cross-country passenger train left Montreal on June 28, 1886. The trip across the country took almost a week. Van Horne knew that people wanted to stop along the way and see the new country. For that reason, the railroad began building hotels along the tracks.

During construction, three CPR workers discovered a natural **hot spring** in the mountains. Van Horne knew it would be a major tourist attraction. He convinced the government to protect the area and allow the Canadian Pacific Railway Company to build a hotel there. This led to the creation of Canada's first national park, which would later be named Banff.

As more and more settlers and tourists travelled west on the railway, the company's business grew. They built more hotels throughout the country and expanded the railway. They hired ships to sail between Canada and Asia, bringing goods like tea and silk to Canadians.

1867   1869   1869–1870   1870–1871   1872–1873   1873–1880

"If we can't export the scenery, we'll import the tourists." William Cornelius Van Horne

The Canadian Pacific Railway led to the construction of a series of grand railway hotels across Canada. The Banff Springs Hotel might be the most recognizable of them all.

The Canadian Pacific Railway is one of the greatest Canadian achievements. It united the new nation of Canada by linking East to West. It opened new lands for discovery. The railway transformed the Canadian landscape, bringing millions of people west to settle and build the country. It even helped make Canada the **multicultural** nation it is today. Many of the Chinese workers who came to build the railroad stayed in Canada, and millions of Europeans came to farm the land.

These workers founded cities and towns across the prairies and mountains. Today, most of Canada's 35 million people still live near CPR routes. Almost 130 years after the railway's completion, CPR continues carrying goods and travellers across the country.

John A. Macdonald's dream of a united Canada was difficult to achieve. He fought rebellions, risked bankruptcy, and even lost his job as prime minister. By being persistent and by relying on help from Canadians and others around the world, he reached his goal. Thanks to the Canadian Pacific Railway, Canada stretches across the continent, united as one nation.

1867   1869   1869–1870   1870–1871   1872–1873   1873–1880

"Without railways there would be and could be no Canada." George Stanley

The Canadian Pacific Railway played a large part in making Canada the country that it is today.

Brain Teaser

1. What prime minister dreamed of uniting Canada with a railway?

2. What four provinces joined Canada on July 1, 1867?

3. What HBC leader negotiated with Louis Riel for the government of Canada in 1870?

4. What province agreed to join Canada in exchange for a railroad?

5. What type of zones did Sandford Fleming help develop?

6. How much money were Chinese workers paid to build the CPR?

7. What event in 1885 convinced the Canadian government to give more money to the CPR?

8. What national park did William Cornelius Van Horne help develop?

ANSWERS

1. John A. Macdonald
2. Ontario, Quebec, New Brunswick, and Nova Scotia
3. Donald Smith
4. British Columbia
5. Time zones
6. $1 per day
7. The North-West Rebellion
8. Banff National Park

Further Information

Learn all about the building of the CPR from this film: www.youtube.com/watch?v=1GDTWT3m2YA

Look at this website to learn more about the construction of the CPR: www.cpr.ca/en/about-cp/our-past-present-and-future/Documents/cp-childrens-history.pdf

Learn more about Chinese CPR workers: www.mhso.ca/tiesthatbind/index.php

Watch this video about Sandford Fleming and standardized time: www.historicacanada.ca/content/heritage-minutes/sir-sandford-fleming?media_type=41&media_category=34

See a dangerous job performed by Chinese CPR workers: www.historicacanada.ca/content/heritage-minutes/nitro?media_type=41&

This timeline tracks the building of railways in Canada: www.railways.incanada.net/candate/candate.htm

Glossary

campaign: an organized effort to win a political competition

colony: land controlled by another country

Confederation: the union of Canada

contract: a deal made by two sides

debt: money owed to someone else

election: a political competition

exile: living in a different country for political reasons

hot spring: a pool of naturally hot water

majority: most

Métis: a nation formed by French fur traders having children with First Nations people

multicultural: a nation made up of many different cultures

negotiate: try to make a deal

opposition party: the political party with the second-most votes

representation: a person or group acting in front of a legislative body on behalf of others

showcase: to display something proudly

spike: a large, pointy piece of metal driven into the ground to hold the railroad in place

time zones: 24 regions around the world, organized for accurate timekeeping

Index